E
Ho

Hoban, Tana
Round and round and round.

TANA HOBAN

Round
&
Round
&
Round

GREENWILLOW BOOKS, NEW YORK

Library of Congress
Cataloging in Publication Data

Hoban, Tana.
Round and round and round.
Summary: Color photos without text
feature objects that are round.
1. Circle—Juvenile literature.
[1. Circle—Pictorial works]   I. Title.
QA484.H628   1983   516'.15   82-11984
ISBN 0-688-01813-0
ISBN 0-688-01814-9 (lib. bdg.)

This one
is especially for John

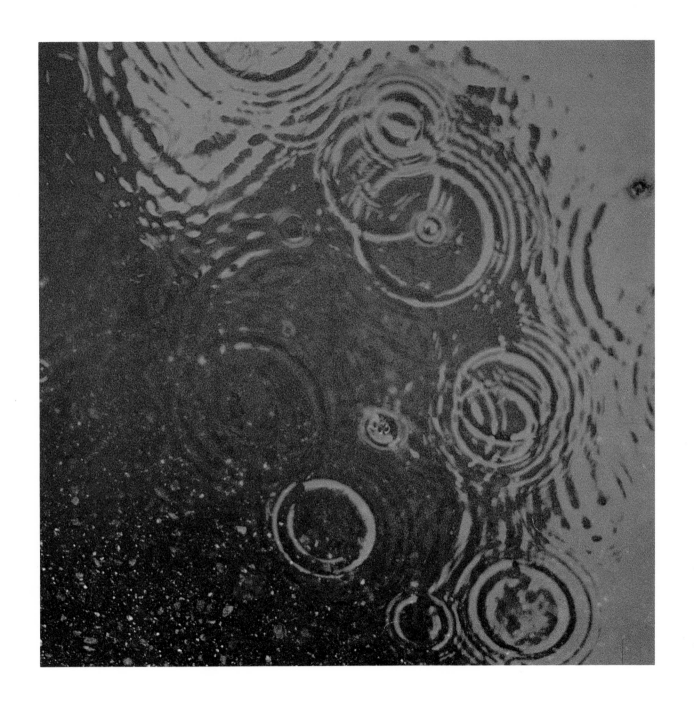

Tana Hoban's photographs have been exhibited at the Museum of Modern Art in New York. She has won many gold medals and prizes for her work as a photographer and filmmaker. And, of course, her books for children are known and loved throughout the world.